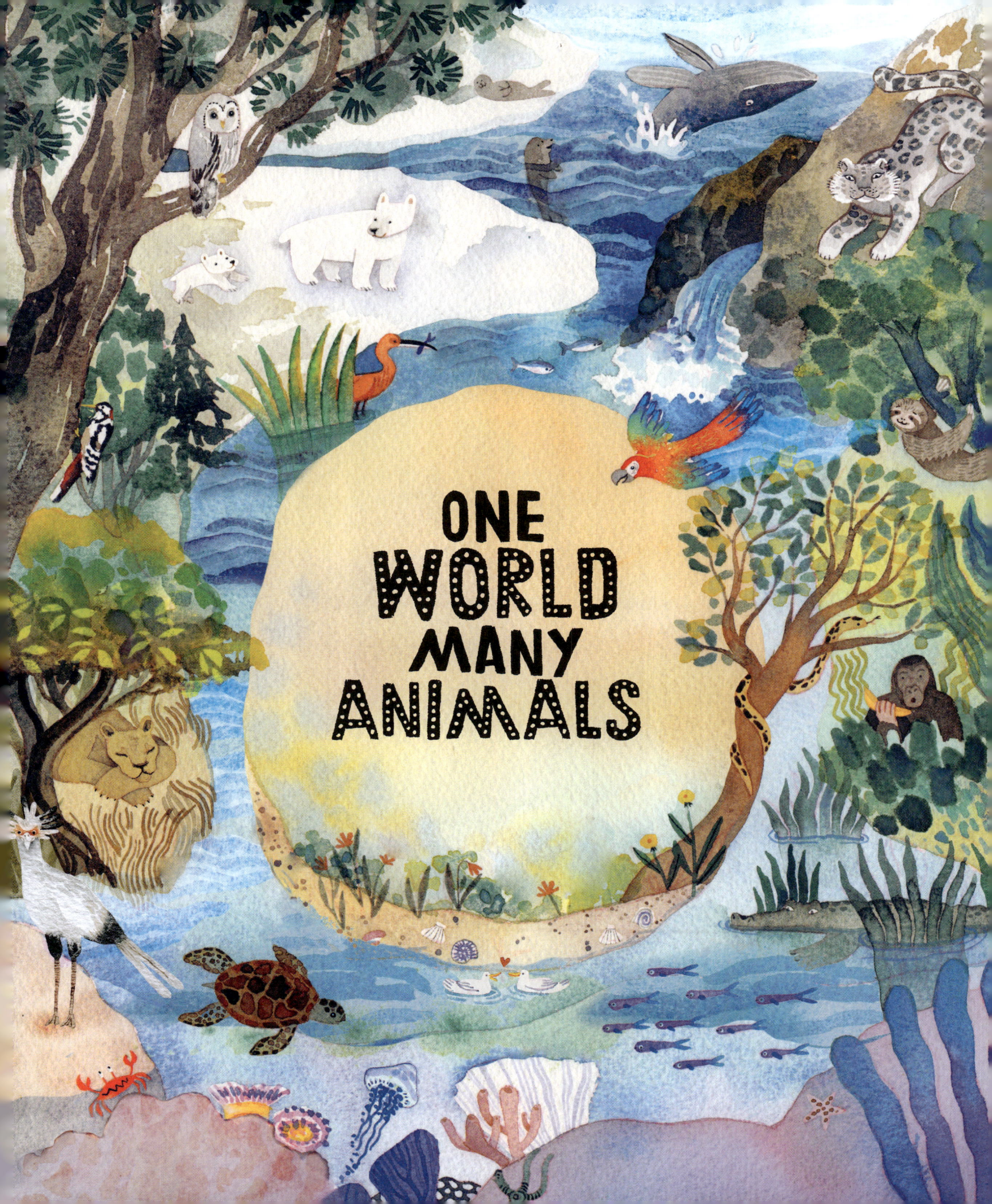

For Theo - B.L.
To Mégane - A.S.

© 2025 Quarto Publishing plc
Text © 2025 Ben Lerwill
Illustrations © 2025 Alette Straathof

First published in 2025 by words & pictures,
an imprint of The Quarto Group.
1 Triptych Place, London,
SE1 9SH, United Kingdom.
T (0)20 7700 6700 F (0)20 7700 8066
www.quarto.com

EEA Representation, WTS Tax d.o.o.,
Žanova ulica 3, 4000 Kranj, Slovenia.

Editor: Alice Hobbs
Designer: Sarah Chapman-Suire
Creative Director: Malena Stojić
Associate Publisher: Holly Willsher
Production Manager: Nikki Ingram

No part of this publication may be reproduced, stored
in a retrieval system, or transmitted in any form, or by any
means, electrical, mechanical, photocopying, recording or
otherwise, without the prior written permission of the publisher
or a licence permitting restricted copying. In the United Kingdom
such licences are issued by the Copyright Licensing Agency,
5th Floor, Shackleton House, 4 Battle Bridge Lane,
London SE1 2HX.

All rights reserved.

A catalogue record for this book is available from the British Library.

ISBN: 978 0 7112 9732 6

9 8 7 6 5 4 3 2 1

Manufactured in Guangdong, China TT022025

# ONE WORLD MANY ANIMALS

Ben Lerwill
Alette Straathof

We share the world with
millions of other animal species.

They live in hot places, cold places, busy places and wild places.

Planet Earth is their home, just like it is our home.

The place where an animal lives – like a jungle, a desert or a river – is called its habitat.

The world is full of different animal habitats, and each one is teeming with different species.

**Are you ready to take a look?**

# What's in the steamy Amazon rainforest?

A **three-toed sloth** hanging from a mossy branch.

A **boa constrictor** wrapped around a branch, watching and waiting.

A **scarlet macaw** swooping through the leafy canopy on rainbow wings.

A **jaguar** creeping through the trees.

## What else can you see?

A red-eyed tree frog?
Two woolly monkeys?
Three vampire bats?
A glittering-bellied emerald hummingbird?

# What's in the big blue sea?

A **humpback whale** diving into the deep.

A **common octopus** travelling along the rocky seabed.

A shoal of **menhaden** fish drifting this way and that.

**Bluefin tuna** swimming, fast and strong.

## What else can you see?

A great blue barracuda?
Pink sea nettle jellyfish?
Two striped bass?
An Atlantic wolffish?

A **common centipede** crawling deep underground.

## What else can you see?

A stag beetle?
A leopard slug?
Four pill woodlice?
Two house mice?

# What's in the hot, sandy desert?

Two **dromedary camels** walking slowly over the dunes.

A **horned viper** slithering over the sand.

Three **dorcas gazelles** chewing at grass.

A **sand cat** padding silently through the dusk.

## What else can you see?

A pharaoh eagle-owl?
A desert monitor lizard?
A long-eared jerboa?
A deathstalker scorpion?

# What's on the wide African plains?

An **elephant** walking slow and steady.

**Bush grasshoppers** jumping from plant to plant like tiny acrobats.

**Barn swallows** speeding through the warm evening air.

A pride of **lions** hidden in the grass, ready to pounce.

## What else can you see?

A secretary bird?
Two termite mounds?
A herd of zebras?
Two warthogs?

# What's in the windy Himalayan mountains?

A **Himalayan vulture** high overhead, scanning the slopes for a meal.

**Goat antelopes** teetering up a steep cliff.

A **snow leopard** crossing the mountainside on thick paws.

A **Himalayan tahr** grazing in the valley, its coat thick and shaggy.

### What else can you see?

A blue whistling thrush?
A jumping spider?
A snow partridge?
Two red pandas?

**Bearded seals** diving for fish in the cold sea.

A **snowy owl**, proud and powerful.

## What else can you see?

A musk ox?
Two snow buntings?
A herd of caribou?
A narwhal?

# What's in the soft, sunny meadow?

Two **collared doves** cooing in the clear morning air.

**Swallowtail butterflies** flip-flapping high and low.

A herd of **red deer** feeding on the grass.

**Garden bumblebees** buzzing from flower to flower.

What else can you see?

Three starlings?
A long-eared hare?
A vole nibbling fruit?
A ring-necked pheasant?

# What's in the tropical coral reef?

A **hawksbill sea turtle** gliding through the blue.

A **common parrotfish** chewing on the coral.

A **pygmy seahorse** bobbing on the tide.

A **honeycomb moray eel** twisting out of a crevice.

## What else can you see?

Two common clownfish?
Five peacock damselfish?
A manta ray?
Two giant clams?

# What's in the dappled green woodland?

A **brown bear** sniffing the cool forest air.

A **weasel** scampering through the oak trees.

**Dragonflies** zipping over the surface of the river.

**Atlantic salmon** swimming through the clear shallows.

What else can you see?

A hawk moth?
A plump waxwing bird?
A common toad?
A woodpecker?

# What's in the splashy rockpool?

A **rockpool blenny** darting through the ripples.

**Beadlet anemones** waving their tentacles in the salty water.

A **common starfish** stretching its five arms along the rocky wall.

A **green shore crab** on the sandy floor.

*What else can you see?*

**Common limpets?
A hermit crab?
Two common gobies?
Three brown shrimp?**

**What's in the big, bustling city?**

Florals

**Seven-spotted ladybirds** looping among the flowers.

A **peregrine falcon**, eyes bright, perched up high.

**Pigeons** pecking and strutting on the pavement.

A **red fox** slipping quietly through the streets.

## What else can you see?

A honeybee?
Two house sparrows?
A garden snail?
A grey squirrel?

And in every one of these habitats, animals **snuffle, swim, soar and sleep**.

The word we use to describe the variety of life in the natural world is 'biodiversity'.

Having so many wonderful creatures living on our planet makes Earth a place of **amazing** biodiversity.

The little and the large, the furry and the feathery, the predators and the prey – all these animals play a part in keeping the natural world in balance.

All of them are part of the great web of life. And all of them are precious.

# A note from the author

Imagine a planet packed with biodiversity. A world where animals live in every corner of the map, from the deepest, darkest forests to the biggest, busiest cities. Some of these animals are tall and some are small. Some can swim and some can fly. Some have lots of eyes and some have no eyes at all! Every single one is important.

We know this world very well, of course, because it's our planet. Planet Earth is big, beautiful and bursting with life. Every single species in our world is special, but there's one animal that has more power than any of the others. That's us – the humans! So let's use that power for good. The world's wildlife deserves the brightest possible future we can give it.

Six ways to help wildlife:

*Pick up litter.* Rubbish can pollute our seas and rivers and interfere with habitats.

*Make your space wild.* If you have a garden, community allotment or windowbox, let some of it grow wild to attract animals.

*Learn more about the wild animals in your local area.* The more you understand how they live, the more you'll enjoy observing and protecting them.

*Recycle.* The more paper and card we recycle, the fewer trees we need to chop down.

*Join a wildlife group.* By becoming part of a local wildlife group or a big international animal charity, you can be even more involved in helping animals.

*Spread the word.* If you're passionate about animals, let your friends and family know – and help them to protect wildlife, too.